MIND OVER EMOTIONS

A JOURNEY TO EMOTIONAL MASTERY AND CONQUERING NEGATIVITY

TABLE OF CONTENTS

Mind over Emotions

Introduction

Understanding the Power of Emotions

  The Importance of Emotional Intelligence

  The Negative Impact of Unmanaged Emotions

  The Benefits of Mastering Your Emotions

Chapter 2

Understanding Your Emotions: The Science of Feelings

  The Brain and Emotion

  Types of Emotions

  The Connection Between Emotions and Thoughts

    The Role of Emotion Regulation

Chapter 3

Overcoming Negativity: How to Break the Cycle of Negative Thinking

  Identifying Negative Thoughts

  Challenging Negative Thoughts

  The Link Between Negativity and Emotions

Chapter 4.

Managing Your Emotions: Techniques for Emotional Control

  Mindfulness and Emotional Self-Awareness

  Techniques for Emotional Control

  The Power of positive thinking

Chapter 5.

Communicating Effectively: Navigating Interpersonal Relationships

  The Role of Emotions in Communication

  Strategies for Managing Difficult Conversations

  Building Stronger Relationships Through Emotional Intelligence

Chapter 6:
Applying Emotional Mastery in Daily Life

Managing Stress and Anxiety
Improving Work and Study Performance
Maintaining Emotional Balance in Relationships
Chapter 7
Conclusion: The Long-Term Benefits of Emotional Mastery
Sustaining emotional intelligence
The Importance of Continuous Learning
The Future of Emotional Mastery
Bonus chapter
Depression, Jealousy And Procrastination
Depression
Jealousy
Procrastination

References
Appendix A: Additional Resources
Appendix B: Exercises and activities

INTRODUCTION
Understanding the Power of Emotions

Emotions are a powerful force that shape our lives in countless ways. They can inspire us to reach for our goals, motivate us to overcome obstacles, and bring us joy and happiness. However, emotions can also be a source of pain and suffering. They can lead to feelings of anger, sadness, and despair, and can make it difficult to cope with the challenges of everyday life.

The ability to understand and manage our emotions is essential for leading a happy and fulfilling life. It allows us to respond to the world around us in a healthy and constructive way, and to build strong and meaningful relationships with others.

In this book, we will explore the nature of emotions and the ways in which they influence our thoughts, behaviors, and relationships. We will examine the latest research on emotions and the brain, and we will learn practical techniques for managing our emotions and achieving greater emotional balance.

Through this book, you will learn how to:

- Understand the nature and functions of emotions
- Recognize and name your emotions
- Identify the triggers of negative emotions
- Develop emotional regulation skills
- Create a positive emotional environment

- Build emotional resilience

This book is a practical guide to mastering your emotions and using them to live a happier, more fulfilling life. Whether you are struggling with emotional difficulties or simply looking to improve your emotional well-being, this book will provide you with the tools and knowledge you need to take control of your emotions and achieve greater emotional balance

THE IMPORTANCE OF EMOTIONAL INTELLIGENCE

Emotional intelligence (EI) is the ability to recognize, understand, and manage our own emotions and the emotions of others. It is a crucial component of overall well-being and success in life. People with high emotional intelligence are able to navigate the complex social landscape of life with greater ease and effectiveness, and they enjoy stronger relationships, more satisfying careers, and better overall mental health.

Emotional intelligence is composed of five key competencies:

- Self-awareness: the ability to recognize and understand one's own emotions
- Self-regulation: the ability to manage and control one's own emotions
- Motivation: the ability to use emotions to achieve goals
- Empathy: the ability to understand and respond to the emotions of others
- Social skills: the ability to build and maintain relationships

In this book, we will explore the importance of emotional intelligence and the ways in which it can be developed and strengthened. We will examine the latest research on emotional intelligence and the brain, and we will learn practical techniques for improving our own emotional intelligence.

Through this book, you will learn how to:

- Recognize and understand emotions
- Develop self-awareness
- Improve self-regulation
- Utilize emotions to achieve goals
- Understand and respond to the emotions of others
- Enhance social skills and build strong relationships

This book will help you to develop and strengthen your emotional intelligence and to use it to achieve greater success in all areas of life. Whether you are looking to improve your relationships, advance in your career, or simply lead a happier and more fulfilling life, this book will provide you with the tools and knowledge you need to succeed.

In addition to the practical benefits of emotional intelligence, it also has a powerful impact on our overall well-being. People with high emotional intelligence are better able to cope with stress and adversity, and they enjoy greater emotional resilience. They are also more likely to experience positive emotions like happiness and contentment, and they are less likely to experience negative emotions like anger, anxiety, and depression.

Furthermore, emotional intelligence plays a crucial role in leadership and management, by allowing leaders to understand the emotions of their team members and to use this understanding to build trust, motivation, and collaboration. It also allows leaders to manage their own emotions, which helps them to make better decisions and to navigate the challenges of leading others.

In summary, emotional intelligence is an essential component of overall well-being, success and a healthy relationships. This book will provide you with a deeper understanding of emotions and the ways in which they influence our thoughts, behaviors, and relationships, as well as the tools you need to master your emotions and use them to achieve greater happiness, success, and well-being.

THE NEGATIVE IMPACT OF UNMANAGED EMOTIONS

Emotions are a powerful force that can have a significant impact on our lives. When managed effectively, they can provide us with energy, motivation, and a sense of purpose. However, when left unmanaged, they can lead to a wide range of negative consequences.

Unmanaged emotions can lead to a host of mental and physical health problems, such as anxiety, depression, and stress-related illnesses. They can also lead to difficulties in personal relationships, as well as problems at work or in school. Negative emotions like anger, fear, and sadness can cloud our judgment and make it difficult to think clearly, while positive emotions can cause us to act impulsively and make poor decisions.

Unmanaged emotions can also lead to addictions, such as over-eating, smoking, drinking and substance abuse, as individuals may use these vices as a way to cope with and suppress their emotions. These addictions can lead to a whole host of physical and mental health issues, as well as financial and societal problems.

Furthermore, unmanaged emotions can lead to a lack of emotional resilience, and may make it more difficult for individuals to cope with difficult situations, resulting in them becoming overwhelmed and unable to function effectively.

In this book, we will explore the negative impacts of unmanaged emotions and the ways in which they can be addressed and overcome. We will examine the latest research on emotions and the brain, and we will learn practical techniques for managing our emotions and achieving greater emotional balance.

Through this book, you will learn how to:

- Recognize and manage negative emotions
- Develop emotional regulation skills
- Identify and avoid emotional triggers
- Build emotional resilience
- Create a positive emotional environment

By learning to manage our emotions more effectively, we can avoid the negative consequences of unmanaged emotions and enjoy greater well-being, success, and happiness in all areas of our lives.

THE BENEFITS OF MASTERING YOUR EMOTIONS

Mastering your emotions means understanding and managing them in a way that enhances your overall well-being and allows you to achieve your goals. It enables you to respond to the world around you in a healthy and constructive way, and to build strong and meaningful relationships with others.

When you master your emotions, you will experience a range of benefits including:

- Improved mental health: By managing your emotions, you reduce the risk of developing mental health issues such as anxiety and depression. You also become more resilient to stress and negative life events.
- Better relationships: When you master your emotions, you become more able to understand and communicate with others, which leads to stronger and more fulfilling relationships.
- Increased productivity: By managing your emotions, you become better able to focus on your tasks and to stay motivated, which leads to greater productivity.
- Greater emotional balance: Mastering your emotions allows you to achieve a greater sense of emotional balance, which leads to greater happiness, satisfaction, and well-being.
- Better decision making: When you master your emotions, you become less prone to impulsivity and

more able to think clearly, which leads to better decision making.

- Improved physical health: Managing your emotions can have a positive impact on your physical health as well, as chronic stress and negative emotions have been linked to various health issues such as high blood pressure, heart disease, and weakened immune system.

Overall, mastering your emotions can bring about significant positive changes in all aspects of your life, from your mental and physical health, to your relationships and career. This book will provide you with the tools and knowledge you need to achieve greater emotional balance and well-being.

In this book, we will explore the different aspects of emotional intelligence and the ways in which it can be developed. We will examine the latest research on emotions and the brain, and we will learn practical techniques for managing our emotions and achieving greater emotional balance.

We will also delve into the specific emotions that can be particularly challenging to manage, such as anger, fear, and sadness, and provide strategies for dealing with these emotions in a healthy and constructive way.

In addition, we will explore the connection between emotions and physical health, and how managing our emotions can help us to maintain a healthy lifestyle.

In summary, mastering your emotions is crucial for achieving greater well-being, success, and happiness in all areas of your life. This book will provide you with a deeper understanding of emotions and the ways in which they influence our thoughts, behaviors, and relationships, as well as the tools you need to master your emotions and use them to achieve greater success and well-being.

CHAPTER 2

Understanding Your Emotions: The Science of Feelings

Emotions play a crucial role in our lives, influencing our thoughts, behaviors, and relationships. But what exactly are emotions and how are they processed in the brain? This chapter will explore the science of emotions, delving into the ways in which emotions are processed in the brain and how they are connected to physical sensations.

THE BRAIN AND EMOTION

Emotions are processed in a network of brain regions, including the amygdala, the prefrontal cortex, and the insula. The amygdala, a small almond-shaped structure located deep in the brain, is responsible for detecting and responding to emotionally-relevant stimuli. When the amygdala perceives a threat, it sends a signal to the body to activate the fight-or-flight response, increasing heart rate, blood pressure and releasing stress hormones.

The prefrontal cortex, located at the front of the brain, is responsible for regulating emotions. It works to inhibit the amygdala's response and modulate the intensity of emotions. The insula, located deep in the brain, is responsible for processing the bodily sensations that accompany emotions, such as the rapid heartbeat associated with fear or the butterflies in the stomach associated with excitement.

TYPES OF EMOTIONS

There are many different types of emotions, including basic emotions such as happiness, sadness, fear, anger, and disgust, as well as more complex emotions like guilt and shame. Basic emotions are thought to be universal across cultures and are typically easy to recognize. They are also thought to have evolved as a means of quickly and efficiently communicating with others.

Theories of Emotion

There are many different theories of emotion, including the James-Lange theory, Cannon-Bard theory, and the Schacter-Singer two-factor theory. The James-Lange theory, proposed in the late 1800s, suggests that emotions are the result of physiological responses to external stimuli. The Cannon-Bard theory, proposed in the 1920s, suggests that emotions and physiological responses occur simultaneously. The Schacter-Singer two-factor theory, proposed in the 1960s, suggests that emotions are the result of the interaction between cognitive appraisals and physiological responses.

Emotion Triggers and Impact on Behaviour

Emotions can be triggered by a wide variety of factors, including external events, thoughts, and memories. They can also be triggered by internal physiological changes, such as hunger or fatigue. Once triggered, emotions can have a significant impact on behaviour. For example, fear can lead to avoidance behaviour, while anger can lead to aggression.

Measuring Emotions

Emotions can be measured in a variety of ways, including self-report measures, physiological measures, and behavioural measures. Self-report measures, such as surveys or questionnaires, rely on individuals to report on their own emotional experiences. Physiological measures, such as heart rate or skin conductance, rely on changes in the body's physiological responses to emotions. Behavioural measures, such as facial expressions or tone of voice, rely on observable changes in behaviour.

Emotions and Mental Health

Emotions also play a significant role in mental health. Research has shown that individuals with certain mental health conditions, such as depression and anxiety, tend to experience emotions more intensely or for longer periods of time. Additionally, individuals with certain mental health conditions may also have difficulty regulating their emotions.

Emotions and Physical Health

Emotions can also impact physical health. Chronic stress, for example, has been linked to a variety of physical health problems, including heart disease and diabetes. Additionally, chronic anger and hostility have been linked to an increased risk of heart disease.

Emotions and Social Relationships

Emotions also play a significant role in social relationships. Research has shown that individuals who are able to effectively manage their emotions tend to have better relationships with others. Additionally, individuals who are able to accurately recognize and respond to the emotions of others tend to have better social relationships.

Emotional Intelligence

Emotional intelligence (EI) refers to the ability to recognize, understand, and manage emotions. Research has shown that individuals with high emotional intelligence tend to be more successful in their personal and professional lives. Additionally, emotional intelligence can be developed and improved through training and practice.

In conclusion, emotions play a significant role in our

lives, influencing our thoughts, behaviours, and relationships. Understanding the science of emotions, including the brain regions involved, the different types of emotions, the theories of emotion, and the impact of emotions on behaviour and health, can help us better understand and manage our own emotions and the emotions of others. Additionally, developing emotional intelligence can lead to greater success in personal and professional life.

THE CONNECTION BETWEEN EMOTIONS AND THOUGHTS

The connection between emotions and thoughts is a complex one. Emotions and thoughts are closely connected, influencing each other in a bidirectional manner.

Emotions can influence thoughts by shaping attention, memory and perception. For example, a person who is feeling anxious may pay more attention to potential threats, remember more negative events, and perceive more danger in ambiguous situations. Additionally, research has shown that emotions can also influence decision-making, with individuals being more likely to make impulsive decisions when they are experiencing strong emotions.

On the other hand, thoughts can also influence emotions. For example, if an individual has negative thoughts about themselves or a situation, they are more likely to experience negative emotions such as sadness or anxiety. Additionally, cognitive reappraisal, which is the process of changing the way we think about a situation, can be used to regulate emotions.

In short, emotions and thoughts are closely connected, influencing each other in a bidirectional manner. Understanding this connection can help us better understand and manage our own emotions, as well as the emotions of others.

The Role of Emotion Regulation

Emotion regulation refers to the process of managing one's emotions in order to achieve a desired outcome. There are several strategies that can be used to regulate emotions, including:

1. Reappraisal: This involves changing the way we think about a situation in order to change the emotional response. For example, reframing a negative experience as a learning opportunity can reduce negative emotions.
2. Suppression: This involves trying to hide or suppress the expression of an emotion. However, research has shown that suppression may lead to negative consequences such as increased physiological arousal and decreased social interactions.
3. Acceptance: This involves accepting and acknowledging the emotion without trying to change it. Research has shown that acceptance can lead to decreased emotional intensity and increased psychological well-being.
4. Distraction: This involves diverting attention away from the emotion-provoking situation. Research has shown that distraction can lead to decreased emotional intensity.

Emotion regulation plays an important role in mental and physical health. For example, individuals who are able to effectively regulate their emotions tend to have better mental health outcomes, such as lower levels of anxiety and depression. Additionally, individuals who are able to effectively regulate their emotions also tend to have better physical health outcomes, such as lower blood pressure and heart rate.

In conclusion, emotions and thoughts are closely connected, influencing each other in a bidirectional manner. Understanding the connection between emotions and thoughts, as well as the role of emotion regulation, can help us better understand and manage our own emotions and the emotions of others. Additionally, it can also lead to better mental and physical health outcomes.

CHAPTER 3

Overcoming Negativity: How to Break the Cycle of Negative Thinking

Negative thinking patterns can be detrimental to mental and physical health, leading to conditions such as depression and anxiety. Additionally, negative thinking patterns can also make it difficult to achieve goals and maintain positive relationships. Understanding how to break the cycle of negative thinking can lead to improved mental and physical health, as well as greater success in personal and professional life.

Identifying Negative Thinking Patterns

The first step in breaking the cycle of negative thinking is to identify negative thinking patterns. Common negative thinking patterns include:

1. All-or-nothing thinking: This involves seeing things in black-and-white terms, with no middle ground.

2. Overgeneralization: This involves making broad generalizations based on a single event.

3. Mental filter: This involves focusing on the negative aspects of a situation and ignoring the positive aspects.

4. Disqualifying the positive: This involves dismissing positive experiences as unimportant.

5. Magnification and minimization: This involves

exaggerating the negative aspects of a situation and minimizing the positive aspects.

6. Catastrophizing: This involves expecting the worst to happen.

Challenging Negative Thinking Patterns

Once negative thinking patterns have been identified, the next step is to challenge them. This can be done by:

1. Asking for evidence: asking for evidence to support the negative thought.

2. Considering alternative perspectives: looking at the situation from different perspectives.

3. Using "what if" thinking: considering the worst-case scenario and the best-case scenario.

4. Practicing mindfulness: being present in the moment and non-judgmental.

5. Engaging in positive self-talk: replacing negative thoughts with positive affirmations.

Negative thinking patterns can be detrimental to mental and physical health. Understanding how to break the cycle of negative thinking, including identifying negative thinking patterns and challenging them, can lead to improved mental and physical health, as well as greater success in personal and professional life.

Creating a Positive Mindset

Breaking the cycle of negative thinking is an ongoing process and requires a consistent effort to maintain a positive mindset. Here are a few strategies that can be used to create a positive mindset:

1. Surrounding oneself with positive people: spending time with positive people can help to improve one's mood and reduce stress.

2. Practicing gratitude: focusing on the things one is

thankful for can help to reduce negative thoughts and increase positive emotions.

3. Engaging in physical activity: regular exercise has been shown to improve mood and reduce stress.

4. Getting enough sleep: lack of sleep can lead to negative thinking patterns and mood swings.

5. Engaging in hobbies and interests: engaging in activities that one enjoys can help to reduce stress and improve mood.

It's important to remember that breaking the cycle of negative thinking is a process, and it takes time and effort. However, by identifying negative thinking patterns, challenging them, and creating a positive mindset, one can lead a happier and more fulfilling life.

In conclusion, negative thinking patterns can have a significant impact on mental and physical health, as well as on personal and professional life. By understanding the negative patterns, challenging them and creating a positive mindset, one can overcome negativity, lead a happier and more fulfilling life.

Identifying Negative Thoughts

Identifying negative thoughts is an important step in breaking the cycle of negative thinking. Negative thoughts can be defined as automatic and often irrational thoughts that can lead to negative emotions, such as anxiety and depression. Negative thoughts can also be limiting and can prevent an individual from achieving their goals and aspirations.

Recognizing Negative Thoughts

Recognizing negative thoughts can be challenging, as they often occur automatically and unconsciously. However, there are a few strategies that can be used to recognize negative thoughts:

1. Keep a thought diary: write down any negative thoughts that come to mind.

2. Identify triggers: pay attention to situations or events that may trigger negative thoughts.

3. Be mindful: be aware of your thoughts and emotions, and try to catch negative thoughts as they occur.

4. Practice self-compassion: be kind and understanding towards yourself when you have negative thoughts.

CHALLENGING NEGATIVE THOUGHTS

Once negative thoughts have been recognized, the next step is to challenge them. This can be done by:

1. Asking yourself if the thought is rational: is the thought based on evidence or is it an assumption?

2. Considering alternative perspectives: looking at the situation from different perspectives.

3. Using positive self-talk: replacing negative thoughts with positive affirmations.

4. Practicing mindfulness: being present in the moment and non-judgmental.

In conclusion, Identifying negative thoughts is an important step in breaking the cycle of negative thinking. Negative thoughts can lead to negative emotions, limit one's potential and prevent an individual from achieving their goals and aspirations. Recognizing negative thoughts and challenging them can be challenging, but with the use of the strategies mentioned above, one can overcome negativity.

THE LINK BETWEEN NEGATIVITY AND EMOTIONS

Negativity and emotions are closely linked. Negative thoughts and emotions can feed off of each other, creating a vicious cycle of negativity that can be difficult to break. Negative thoughts can lead to negative emotions, such as anxiety and depression. These negative emotions can then lead to more negative thoughts, further perpetuating the cycle.

Negativity and emotions can also interact in a physical way. Negative thoughts and emotions can activate the body's stress response, releasing stress hormones such as cortisol and adrenaline. These hormones can have a number of negative effects on the body, including increasing the risk of heart disease, stroke and other health problems.

Breaking the Cycle

Breaking the cycle of negativity and emotions can be challenging, but it is possible. One of the most effective ways to break the cycle is by learning to recognize negative thoughts and emotions and then challenging and replacing them with positive thoughts and emotions. This can be done by using techniques such as cognitive behavioral therapy, mindfulness, and positive self-talk.

It is important to note that it is not about repressing or denying negative emotions, but rather learning to process and manage them in a healthy way. By managing our emotions, we can reduce the impact of negativity on our lives and improve our overall well-being.

In conclusion, the link between negativity and emotions is a close one. Negative thoughts and emotions can feed off of each other, creating a vicious cycle of negativity that can be difficult to break. Breaking the cycle of negativity and emotions can be challenging, but it is possible by learning to recognize negative thoughts and emotions and then challenging and replacing them with positive thoughts and emotions.

CHAPTER 4.

Managing Your Emotions: Techniques for Emotional Control

Managing emotions is a crucial part of mastering your emotions. Emotional control is the ability to regulate and control your emotions in a healthy way. It allows you to respond to situations in a calm and rational manner, rather than being controlled by your emotions.

There are a number of techniques that can be used to manage emotions, including:

1. Breathing techniques: slow, deep breathing can help to calm the mind and body.
2. Mindfulness: being present in the moment and non-judgmental can help to reduce the impact of negative emotions.
3. Positive self-talk: replacing negative thoughts with positive affirmations can help to improve mood.
4. Cognitive behavioral therapy: this therapy can help to change negative thought patterns and improve emotional regulation.
5. Relaxation techniques: such as yoga, meditation and massage can help to reduce stress and improve emotional regulation.
6. Exercise: regular exercise has been shown to reduce stress and improve mood.

It is important to note that managing your emotions takes time and practice. It is not a one-time solution but a continuous effort. Finding the right techniques for you and making them a part of your daily routine can help to improve emotional regulation and overall well-being.

- Identifying triggers: Understanding what triggers your negative emotions can help you to anticipate and prepare for them.
- Emotional labeling: Being able to name and identify your emotions can help you to process and understand them better.
- Reframing: Changing the way you think about a situation can change the way you feel about it.
- Empathy: Putting yourself in someone else's shoes can help you to understand and manage your emotions in relation to them.
- Positive visualization: picturing a positive outcome can help to change your mindset and reduce negative emotions.

It is also important to mention that some people may require professional help to manage their emotions. Seeking therapy or counseling can be beneficial for some individuals.

It's important to try different techniques and find what works best for you. Everyone has different needs and preferences, so it's important to be open-minded and willing to experiment with different strategies. Remember that managing emotions is a lifelong journey, and it's okay to not have all the answers or perfect solutions. With time and practice, you can learn to manage your emotions in a healthy way

MINDFULNESS AND EMOTIONAL SELF-AWARENESS

Mindfulness is the practice of being present in the moment and non-judgmentally observing one's thoughts, feelings and surroundings. Mindfulness can help to reduce the impact of negative emotions by allowing individuals to step back and observe their emotions without becoming caught up in them.

Emotional self-awareness is the ability to recognize and understand one's own emotions. It is the foundation for emotional regulation and management. By understanding our emotions and their causes, we can take steps to manage them in a healthy way.

Mindfulness and emotional self-awareness practices can be combined to improve emotional management. For example, a mindfulness exercise like deep breathing or meditation can be used to become more aware of one's emotions and learn to observe them without getting caught up in them. Emotional self-awareness can also be developed by journaling, reflecting on one's emotions and self-reflection.

Additionally, mindfulness-based interventions like Mindfulness-Based Stress Reduction (MBSR) and Acceptance and Commitment Therapy (ACT) have been shown to be effective in increasing emotional self-awareness and managing negative emotions.

It's important to note that developing mindfulness and emotional self-awareness takes time and practice. Consistency is key, so it's important to make these practices a part of your daily routine. With time and practice, you will be able to recognize and understand your emotions better, and ultimately manage them more effectively.

TECHNIQUES FOR EMOTIONAL CONTROL

1. Opposite Action: This strategy involves taking actions that are opposite to the emotions you are feeling. For example, if you are feeling angry, you might try to engage in activities that promote calmness such as yoga or meditation.
2. Refocus: This strategy involves redirecting your attention away from the source of negative emotions and onto something else. For example, if you are feeling stressed at work, you might try going for a walk or listening to music.
3. Reappraise: This strategy involves changing the way you think about a situation in order to change the way you feel about it. For example, instead of thinking "I can't do this," you might try thinking "I can do this, it just might be challenging."
4. Self-Soothe: This strategy involves using soothing activities to calm yourself down when you are feeling upset. For example, you might try taking a warm bath or listening to calming music.
5. Emotion-Focused coping: This strategy involves accepting and dealing with the emotions you are feeling rather than trying to suppress or change them. For example, you might try talking to a friend or writing about your feelings in a journal.
6. Emotion-regulation plan: This strategy involves setting a plan that you can use to manage your emotions. This

plan should include a list of strategies that you can use to manage your emotions when you are feeling upset.

It's important to note that different strategies work for different people, so it's important to experiment with different strategies to find what works best for you. Remember that managing emotions is an ongoing process, and it's okay to not have all the answers or perfect solutions. With time and practice, you can learn to manage your emotions in a healthy way.

THE POWER OF POSITIVE THINKING

Positive thinking is the practice of focusing on positive thoughts and emotions and avoiding negative ones. Positive thinking can help to reduce the impact of negative emotions by allowing individuals to focus on the good things in their lives.

Research has shown that positive thinking can have a range of benefits, including:

- Improving mood and reducing feelings of depression and anxiety
- Improving self-esteem and self-confidence
- Improving overall well-being and life satisfaction
- Improving the immune system and reducing the risk of illness
- Improving problem-solving skills and decision-making abilities
- Improving relationships and social interactions

Some ways to practice positive thinking include:

- Focusing on the present moment and the good things in your life
- Writing down things you're grateful for each day
- Practicing positive self-talk
- Setting positive and realistic goals
- Surrounding yourself with positive people
- Practicing mindfulness and self-reflection

It's important to note that positive thinking is not about ignoring or denying negative emotions or situations. Rather, it's about finding a balance between the positive and negative aspects of life. Positive thinking is a skill that can be developed with practice and effort.

- Positive thinking can lead to an increase in self-motivation and self-discipline, as individuals are more likely to set and achieve goals when they have a positive outlook.
- Positive thinking can lead to increased resilience and the ability to handle stress and adversity more effectively, as individuals are better able to cope with difficult situations when they have a positive mindset.
- Positive thinking can lead to improved physical health, as it has been linked to lower blood pressure, reduced risk of heart disease, and improved immune function.
- Positive thinking can lead to improved relationships, as individuals with a positive mindset tend to be more empathetic and compassionate towards others, which can foster deeper connections and stronger bonds.
- Positive thinking can lead to improved performance in work and school, as individuals with a positive mindset tend to be more productive, focused, and motivated.

It's also important to note that positive thinking is not just about thinking happy thoughts or denying reality. Positive thinking is about finding the balance between the positive and negative aspects of life and learning how to focus on the positive in order to improve overall well-being.

CHAPTER 5.

Communicating Effectively: Navigating Interpersonal Relationships

Effective communication is a key component in navigating interpersonal relationships. It involves the ability to express oneself clearly and effectively, as well as the ability to actively listen and understand the perspectives of others.

Effective communication can help to:

- Build trust and intimacy in relationships
- Resolve conflicts and misunderstandings
- Increase mutual understanding and cooperation
- Improve overall communication and relationship satisfaction

There are several techniques that can be used to improve communication, such as:

- Active listening: This involves fully focusing on and understanding what the other person is saying, rather than simply waiting for your turn to speak.
- Reflective listening: This involves restating or summarizing what the other person has said, to ensure that you have understood them correctly.
- "I" statements: This involves expressing your own feelings and perspectives using "I" statements, rather than blaming or accusing the other person.
- Nonverbal communication: This includes things like body language, facial expressions, and tone of voice, which can convey important information and emotions in addition to spoken words.

- Empathy: This means trying to understand and share the feelings of others, it's a key aspect of understanding where the other person is coming from and being able to respond in a way that is supportive and understanding.
- Assertiveness: This means being able to stand up for yourself and express your needs and wants in an honest and direct way, without being aggressive or passive.

It's important to keep in mind that effective communication is a skill that can be developed and improved over time with practice. It is also important to be aware that communication can be influenced by cultural, social and personal factors. Being aware of these factors can help to improve understanding and reduce misunderstandings.

In summary, effective communication is crucial for navigating interpersonal relationships and can lead to more positive and fulfilling connections with others. The use of techniques such as active listening, reflective listening, "I" statements, nonverbal communication, empathy and assertiveness can be effective in improving communication.

- It is important to remember that effective communication is not just about speaking, but also about listening. Listening actively and attentively is a key component of effective communication, as it allows you to understand and respond to the needs and perspectives of others.
- It is also important to recognize that communication is not always verbal. Nonverbal communication, such as body language, facial expressions, and tone of voice, can also convey important information and emotions. Being aware of nonverbal cues can help you to better understand the messages that others are sending, and to communicate more effectively.
- It's important to be aware of communication styles and preferences, some people prefer to have a direct conversation and others prefer to have a more indirect conversation. Understanding how others prefer to communicate can help to reduce misunderstandings and improve communication.
- Emotional intelligence is also an important aspect of

effective communication. Being aware of your own emotions and how they affect your communication, as well as being able to read and understand the emotions of others, can help to improve communication and navigate interpersonal relationships more effectively.

- It's important to be aware of cultural differences, as communication styles and norms can vary greatly between cultures. Being aware of cultural differences can help to avoid misunderstandings and improve cross-cultural communication.
- Flexibility is also important when it comes to communication. Being able to adapt your communication style to different situations and people can help to improve communication and build better relationships.
- In addition to these points, it's also important to work on developing good conflict resolution skills, as conflicts are an inevitable part of any relationship. Learning how to handle conflicts in a constructive and healthy way can help to improve communication and strengthen relationships.

In conclusion, effective communication is a crucial aspect of interpersonal relationships and can be improved through the use of various techniques, such as active listening, reflective listening, "I" statements, nonverbal communication, empathy, assertiveness and cultural awareness. Additionally, developing emotional intelligence, flexibility and conflict resolution skills can also greatly improve communication and relationships.

THE ROLE OF EMOTIONS IN COMMUNICATION

Emotions play a significant role in communication, they can affect how we express ourselves and how we interpret the messages of others. Emotions can also influence the type of communication we choose to engage in, whether it's verbal or nonverbal.

Positive emotions such as happiness and excitement tend to facilitate communication, making it more open and effective, whereas negative emotions such as anger and frustration can make communication more difficult, leading to misunderstandings or even conflicts.

Emotions can also be conveyed nonverbally, through facial expressions, tone of voice, and body language. Being aware of these nonverbal cues can help to improve understanding and reduce misunderstandings.

Emotions can also play a role in how we interpret and respond to the messages of others. For example, if someone is feeling sad, they may interpret a neutral message as negative, whereas if they are feeling happy, they may interpret the same message as positive.

Moreover, Emotional intelligence (EI) can also greatly influence communication. People with high EI tend to be better able to understand and manage their own emotions, as well as the emotions of others. This can lead to better communication and more positive relationships.

In summary, emotions play a significant role in communication and can greatly influence how we express ourselves, how we interpret messages, and how we navigate relationships. Developing emotional intelligence and being aware of emotions, nonverbal cues, and cultural differences can help to improve communication and build more positive relationships.

- Emotions can act as cues that signal the importance of a message. For example, if someone is expressing a message with a lot of enthusiasm and energy, we may interpret that message as more important or urgent than a message delivered in a monotone voice.
- Emotions can also act as a filter that shapes the way we perceive and process information. For example, if we are feeling anxious, we may be more likely to focus on negative or threatening information, whereas if we are feeling happy, we may be more likely to focus on positive or rewarding information.
- Emotions also play a role in decision making, people tend to make decisions that align with their current emotional state, which could lead to irrational decisions.
- Furthermore, Emotions can also impact the quality and effectiveness of communication. When people are in a positive emotional state, they are more likely to engage in active listening, express empathy and be more open to new ideas. On the other hand, when people are in a negative emotional state, they are more likely to engage in defensive listening, express criticism, and be closed off to new ideas.
- Self-awareness of emotions is crucial in communication, it allows individuals to manage their emotional state, to be aware of how it is impacting their communication and to adjust their communication style to better suit the situation and person they are communicating with.

Overall, emotions play a complex and multifaceted role in communication, they can act as cues, filters, and drivers that shape how we express ourselves, how we interpret messages, and how we navigate relationships. Being aware of the role of emotions in communication and developing emotional intelligence can greatly enhance communication and improve relationships.

STRATEGIES FOR MANAGING DIFFICULT CONVERSATIONS

Managing difficult conversations can be challenging, but there are several strategies that can help to make them more productive and less stressful. Here are a few examples:

- Prepare beforehand: Before engaging in a difficult conversation, take some time to think about what you want to say and how you want to say it. Consider the other person's perspective and try to anticipate any objections or challenges that may arise.
- Set the right tone: Begin the conversation in a calm and respectful manner, and try to avoid using accusatory language or tone.
- Listen actively: Encourage the other person to share their thoughts and feelings by actively listening to what they have to say. Repeat back what they have said to show that you understand and acknowledge their perspective.
- Stay focused on the issue: Try to stay focused on the specific issue at hand and avoid getting sidetracked by unrelated issues or personal attacks.
- Find common ground: Look for areas of agreement and try to build on those to find a mutually acceptable solution.
- Use "I" statements: Speak from your own perspective and use "I" statements to express your thoughts and feelings, rather than making accusations or accusations.
- Take a break if necessary: If the conversation becomes too heated or emotional, take a break to calm down and

regroup. You can then come back to the conversation later with a clearer head.

- Seek professional help: If you feel that the conversation is too difficult to handle on your own, consider seeking the help of a professional mediator or counselor.

In summary, managing difficult conversations requires preparation, active listening, staying focused on the issue, finding common ground, and using "I" statements. It also requires the ability to remain calm and take a break if needed. And if it's needed, seeking professional help. With these strategies, difficult conversations can become more productive and less stressful.

There are several other strategies that can be helpful when navigating difficult conversations. Here are a few more examples:

- Use assertive language: Speak clearly and directly, and avoid using passive or aggressive language. Be assertive in expressing your thoughts and feelings, while still remaining respectful of the other person's perspective.
- Be willing to compromise: Be open to alternative solutions or compromise, rather than insisting on your own way.
- Choose the right time and place: Consider the best time and place to have the conversation, where you will have privacy and minimal distractions.
- Avoid blaming and accusing: Try to avoid placing blame or making accusations, as this can make the other person defensive and less likely to listen to your perspective.
- Take responsibility for your own emotions: Recognize that your own emotions are your responsibility, and try not to let them take control of the conversation.
- Practice empathy: Try to put yourself in the other person's shoes and understand their perspective. This can help to build rapport and find common ground.
- Use humor: Humor can be a powerful tool for diffusing tension and building a more positive and productive conversation.
- Be open to feedback: Be open to feedback, even if it's negative, and use it as an opportunity to learn and grow.

In summary, some additional strategies for managing difficult conversations include using assertive language, being willing to compromise, choosing the right time and place, avoiding blaming and accusing, taking responsibility for your own emotions, practicing empathy, using humour and being open to feedback. These strategies can help to make difficult conversations more productive, less stressful, and more positive.

BUILDING STRONGER RELATIONSHIPS THROUGH EMOTIONAL INTELLIGENCE

Building stronger relationships through emotional intelligence is about developing the ability to understand and manage your own emotions, as well as the emotions of others. This can help to create more positive and effective communication, and ultimately build stronger relationships. Here are a few ways emotional intelligence can help to build stronger relationships:

1. Improved Communication: Emotionally intelligent individuals are better able to understand and communicate their own emotions, as well as the emotions of others. This can help to create more effective communication, as well as reduce misunderstandings and conflicts.

2. Increased Empathy: Emotional intelligence allows individuals to understand and empathize with others, which can help to build trust and deeper connections.

3. Better Conflict Resolution: Emotionally intelligent individuals are better able to navigate and resolve conflicts in a healthy and productive way.

4. Stronger Social Support: Emotionally intelligent

individuals tend to have more positive and supportive relationships, which can be beneficial for both mental and physical well-being.

5. Improved Teamwork: Emotionally intelligent individuals are better able to work effectively in teams, and can help to create a positive and productive work environment.

6. Greater Self-awareness: Greater self-awareness is a key aspect of emotional intelligence, and it allows individuals to understand their own emotions better, which can help to improve overall emotional well-being.

7. More Positive Attitude: Emotionally intelligent individuals tend to have a more positive attitude and outlook on life, which can be beneficial for both personal and professional relationships.

Emotional intelligence plays an important role in building stronger relationships by improving communication, increasing empathy, better conflict resolution, stronger social support, improved teamwork and greater self-awareness. Emotionally intelligent people have a more positive attitude which can lead to better personal and professional relationships.

There are a number of ways to further explore and deepen the understanding of how emotional intelligence can help to build stronger relationships. Here are a few ideas:

1. **Case studies:** Look at specific examples of how individuals or organizations have used emotional intelligence to build stronger relationships. This could include researching examples from personal relationships, business partnerships, or team dynamics.

2. **Research studies:** Review existing research on the topic of emotional intelligence and relationships to gain a deeper understanding of the mechanisms and processes at play.

3. **Personal reflection:** Reflect on your own experiences with relationships and emotional intelligence. Think about how your own emotional intelligence (or lack

thereof) has affected your relationships in the past, and consider how developing your emotional intelligence could improve your relationships going forward.

4. **Interviews:** Interview individuals who have experience with emotional intelligence and relationships, such as therapists, coaches, or leaders in organizations known for their strong relationships.

5. **Practical application:** Try using some of the techniques and strategies for building stronger relationships through emotional intelligence in your own life. This could include things like mindfulness practices, emotional self-awareness exercises, or communication skills training.

6. **Empirical research:** Conduct a study to test the effects of emotional intelligence on the strength of relationships by measuring the emotional intelligence of a group of people and observing their relationships over time.

CHAPTER 6:
Applying Emotional Mastery in Daily Life

Emotional intelligence is not just about understanding emotions, but also about managing them effectively in order to improve overall well-being and relationships. In this chapter, we will explore practical strategies for applying emotional mastery in daily life.

Developing a Daily Practice

One of the most important steps in mastering your emotions is to develop a consistent practice for emotional management. This might include setting aside time each day for mindfulness exercises, journaling, or practicing self-reflection. The key is to find a practice that works for you and make it a consistent part of your daily routine.

Setting Specific, Measurable Goals

Another important step in mastering your emotions is to set specific, measurable goals for improving your emotional intelligence. This might include goals such as reducing stress, improving relationships, or increasing self-awareness. By setting specific, measurable goals, you can track your progress over time and make adjustments as needed.

Physical Health

Managing emotions can have a positive impact on physical health. Chronic stress can lead to a variety of physical symptoms, such as headaches, fatigue, and even chronic illnesses. By managing emotions effectively, you can reduce stress and improve overall physical health.

Handling Difficult Situations

Difficult situations, such as conflicts in relationships or dealing with a difficult boss, can arise in both
personal and professional life. In this section, the author may discuss strategies for managing difficult conversations, such as active listening, staying calm, and expressing oneself assertively. It may also provide tips on how to handle challenging emotions that come up in these situations, such as anger or frustration, in a constructive way.

Integrating Emotional Intelligence into Different Aspects of Life

Emotional intelligence can be applied in many areas of life, such as parenting, leadership, and teamwork. The author may provide guidance on how to integrate emotional intelligence into these different aspects of life, such as setting boundaries and clear communication in parenting, or fostering a positive and productive team culture in the workplace.

By following the strategies discussed in this chapter, readers will be able to apply emotional mastery in daily life and improve their overall well-being and relationships.

Some additional cues that could be noted include:

1. **Coping with Emotional Triggers:** Discussing specific strategies for identifying and managing emotional triggers, such as journaling or finding a healthy outlet for emotions.

2. **Emotional Self-Care:** Exploring the importance of self-care and providing practical tips for integrating self-care into daily life, such as taking regular breaks and setting healthy boundaries.

3. **Emotionally Intelligent Decision Making:** Discussing the role of emotions in decision making and providing strategies for making decisions that are grounded in emotional intelligence.

4. **Emotionally Intelligent Parenting:** Providing guidance on how to use emotional intelligence to improve parenting skills and foster healthy relationships with children.

5. **Emotionally Intelligent Leadership:** Discussing the role of emotional intelligence in leadership and providing strategies for developing emotionally intelligent leadership skills.

6. **Emotionally Intelligent Teamwork:** Exploring how emotional intelligence can improve teamwork and collaboration in the workplace.

7. **Emotionally Intelligent Communication:** Providing guidance on how to communicate effectively and use emotional intelligence to build better relationships with others.

8. **Emotionally Intelligent Conflict Resolution:** Discussing the role of emotional intelligence in resolving conflicts and providing strategies for managing conflicts in a constructive and emotionally intelligent way.

9. **Emotionally Intelligent Time Management:** Providing strategies for managing time and energy in a way that prioritizes emotional well-being and reduces stress.

10. **Emotionally Intelligent Goal Setting:** Discussing how to set goals that are aligned with our values and emotional needs, and providing strategies for staying motivated and on track towards achieving these goals.

11. **Emotionally Intelligent Stress Management:** Exploring the impact of stress on emotions and providing strategies for managing stress in a way that preserves emotional well-being.

12. **Emotionally Intelligent Relationship Building:** Providing guidance on how to build and maintain healthy relationships by using emotional intelligence skills such as empathy, active listening, and effective communication.

MANAGING STRESS AND ANXIETY

Managing stress and anxiety is a process of identifying the sources of stress in your life and developing coping strategies to deal with them. Managing stress and anxiety can be challenging, but there are several strategies that can help. Some of these strategies include:

1. **Exercise:** Regular physical activity can help reduce stress and anxiety by releasing endorphins, which are chemicals in the brain that promote feelings of well-being. 2.

2. **Identifying sources of stress:** This can include things like work, family, relationships, health, and financial issues. By identifying the sources of stress in your life, you can develop strategies to deal with them.

3. **Developing coping strategies:** Once you have identified the sources of stress, you can develop strategies to deal with them. Some strategies include time management, relaxation techniques, exercise, social support, therapy, and healthy eating.

4. **Relaxation Techniques:** Relaxation techniques such as deep breathing, yoga, and meditation can help calm the mind and reduce stress and anxiety.

5. **Time Management:** Prioritizing tasks, setting realistic goals, and scheduling time for activities that you enjoy can help reduce stress and anxiety by reducing feelings of overwhelm.

6. **Social Support:** Surrounding yourself with supportive

friends and family can provide emotional support and reduce stress and anxiety.

7. **Therapy:** Talking to a therapist or counselor can help you learn coping strategies and techniques for managing stress and anxiety.

8. **Nutrition:** Eating a healthy diet that includes plenty of fruits, vegetables, and whole grains can help improve your overall health and reduce stress and anxiety.

9. **Sleep:** Getting enough sleep is important for maintaining emotional well-being and can help reduce stress and anxiety.

It's important to note that everyone is different and what works for one person might not work for another, so it's essential to find what works for you. It's also important to seek professional help if you feel that your stress and anxiety are overwhelming and interfering with your daily life.

IMPROVING WORK AND STUDY PERFORMANCE

In today's fast-paced world, it is essential to have a good work and study performance. Whether you are a student, a professional, or a business owner, you need to be able to manage your time, stay focused, and achieve your goals. This chapter aims to provide you with practical tips and strategies for improving your work and study performance.

The Importance of Emotional Intelligence for Work and Study:

Emotional intelligence (EI) is the ability to recognize, understand, and manage our own emotions, as well as the emotions of others. It plays a crucial role in work and study performance as it allows individuals to be more self-aware, empathetic, and resilient. High EI individuals tend to be more successful in their careers and academics, as they are able to navigate complex social situations and adapt to changing environments.

The Negative Impact of Unmanaged Emotions on Work and Study:

Unmanaged emotions can negatively impact work and study performance. Negative emotions such as anxiety, stress, and anger can lead to poor decision-making, lack of motivation, and difficulty in concentration. Therefore, it is essential to learn how to manage emotions effectively to improve work and study performance.

Techniques for Emotional Control:
There are various techniques that can be used to control emotions and improve work and study performance. Mindfulness and emotional self-awareness practices such as meditation and journaling can help individuals to better understand and regulate their emotions. Additionally, cognitive-behavioral therapy (CBT) techniques such as reframing negative thoughts and positive affirmations can.

Individuals with high EI tend to be more successful in their careers and academics, as they are able to navigate complex social situations and adapt to changing environments.

Another way to improve work and study performance is to learn how to manage stress and anxiety effectively. Stress and anxiety can negatively impact performance by causing difficulty in concentration, lack of motivation, and poor decision-making. There are various techniques that can be used to manage stress and anxiety, such as mindfulness and emotional self-awareness practices, cognitive-behavioral therapy (CBT) techniques, and physical exercise.

Another technique to improve work and study performance is to prioritize and manage time effectively. It's important to set clear goals and prioritize tasks in order to make the most of the time available. This can also be helped by breaking down large tasks into smaller, manageable chunks and using a to-do list or planner to stay organized.

Finally, it can be helpful to seek out feedback and support from colleagues, mentors, and teachers. This can provide valuable insights and guidance, as well as the opportunity to learn from others' experiences and successes.

Improving work and study performance is a multi-faceted process that can be approached in different ways depending on an individual's specific needs. However, some additional strategies that can be used to improve performance include:

    1. Setting clear and achievable goals: This helps

individuals stay focused and motivated, and provides a sense of direction and purpose.

2. Building a positive mindset: Positive thinking and visualization can help individuals overcome negative thoughts and beliefs, and boost confidence and motivation.

3. Managing time effectively: Time management strategies such as setting priorities, breaking down tasks, and using a planner can help individuals stay organized and focused on the most important tasks.

4. Building a support network: Surrounding yourself with supportive people who can provide encouragement and guidance can help individuals stay motivated and on track.

5. Staying physically and mentally healthy: Regular exercise, healthy eating, and getting enough sleep can all help individuals perform better at work and in their studies. Additionally, practicing stress-reducing techniques such as meditation or yoga can help individuals stay calm and focused under pressure.

6. Continuously learning and developing new skills: Keeping up to date with industry trends, reading relevant books and articles, and taking courses or workshops can help individuals stay relevant and improve their performance.

MAINTAINING EMOTIONAL BALANCE IN RELATIONSHIPS

Maintaining emotional balance in relationships can be a challenging task, but it is crucial for the health and longevity of any partnership. One key aspect of this is being aware of your own emotions and how they affect your interactions with others. This includes understanding your triggers, or the things that cause you to react emotionally, as well as learning how to manage and regulate your emotions in a healthy way. Additionally, it's important to be able to communicate effectively with your partner and work together to find solutions to any conflicts that may arise. This may include learning how to compromise, set boundaries, and practice active listening.

Another important aspect of maintaining emotional balance in relationships is understanding and accepting the emotions of your partner. This means being able to empathize with their feelings and perspectives, even if they are different from your own. It also means being able to validate and support your partner's emotions, rather than dismissing or invalidating them. This can help to create a sense of trust and understanding in the relationship, which is crucial for maintaining emotional balance.

It's also important to be aware of the role that external factors can play in relationships, such as stress and fatigue. Being able to identify and address these factors can help prevent them from negatively impacting your emotional balance. This may include making time for self-care, setting realistic expectations, and seeking professional help if needed.

Here a few thing of practice to ensure healthy relationships

1. Understanding the role of emotions in relationships: It's important to recognize that emotions play a significant role in how we interact with others. Understanding our own emotions and how they affect our behavior can help us navigate relationships more effectively.

2. Communicating effectively: Clear and open communication is key to maintaining emotional balance in relationships. This means being able to express our needs, feelings, and boundaries in a healthy and non-confrontational way.

3. Setting healthy boundaries: Setting boundaries is crucial for maintaining emotional balance in relationships. It's important to be clear about what we're comfortable with and what we're not, and to communicate this to others in a respectful and assertive way.

4. Practicing empathy: Putting ourselves in the other person's shoes and trying to understand their perspective can help us approach conflicts and disagreements in a more constructive way.

5. Managing conflict: Disagreements and conflicts are an inevitable part of any relationship. Learning how to manage these conflicts in a healthy way, such as through active listening, compromise, and forgiveness, can help us maintain emotional balance.

6. Prioritizing self-care: It's important to take care of ourselves emotionally, mentally and physically in order to maintain emotional balance in relationships. This means setting aside time for self-reflection, relaxation, and activities that bring us joy.

Overall, maintaining emotional balance in relationships requires a combination of self-awareness, effective communication, and mutual understanding and support. It is a continuous process and requires constant effort, but with the right approach, it can lead to a happier, healthier and more fulfilling relationship

CHAPTER 7
Conclusion: The Long-Term Benefits of Emotional Mastery

The long-term benefits of emotional mastery are numerous and far-reaching. By learning how to identify and manage our emotions, we can lead more fulfilling and satisfying lives. Through the techniques and strategies outlined in this book, we can improve our decision-making, communication skills, and relationships.

One of the most significant benefits of emotional mastery is the ability to overcome negativity and negative thinking patterns. Negative thoughts and emotions can lead to a cycle of self-doubt and self-destructive behavior. By learning how to break this cycle and replace negative thoughts with positive ones, we can lead a more optimistic and productive life.

Emotional mastery also leads to better communication skills, which is essential for building and maintaining healthy relationships. Being able to understand and express our emotions in a healthy way allows us to connect with others on a deeper level and to resolve conflicts more effectively.

Furthermore, Emotional mastery can also improve our work and study performance. When we are able to manage our emotions, we can focus better, think more clearly, and make better decisions. This leads to increased productivity and success in our professional and academic pursuits.

In conclusion, mastering our emotions is a lifelong journey, but the rewards are well worth the effort. By learning how to identify, understand, and manage our emotions, we can lead happier and more fulfilling lives.

SUSTAINING EMOTIONAL INTELLIGENCE

Sustaining emotional intelligence is an ongoing process that requires consistent effort and commitment. To maintain emotional intelligence, it's important to continue developing self-awareness, emotional regulation, and empathy. This can be achieved through various practices such as mindfulness, journaling, and therapy. Additionally, regularly reflecting on past experiences and learning from them can help to improve emotional intelligence in the long-term. Additionally, it's important to surround oneself with supportive people who can provide feedback and encouragement. By consistently working on emotional intelligence, one can experience the long-term benefits of emotional mastery, such as improved relationships, better decision-making, and greater overall well-being.

THE IMPORTANCE OF CONTINUOUS LEARNING

The importance of continuous learning in the context of emotional intelligence cannot be overstated. Emotional intelligence is not a fixed trait, but rather a set of skills that can be developed and strengthened over time. By continuously learning and practicing new strategies for managing emotions and interacting with others, one can improve their emotional intelligence. This can be done through reading and educating oneself on the subject, attending workshops or seminars, and seeking out mentorship or coaching. Additionally, by continually seeking out new experiences and perspectives, one can expand their emotional intelligence. Furthermore, it is important to be open to feedback and willing to change and adjust strategies if they are not working. In this way, continuous learning and self-reflection will help one to progress towards a more emotionally intelligent and fulfilled life.

THE FUTURE OF EMOTIONAL MASTERY

The future of emotional mastery is a topic of much interest and debate among experts in the field of psychology and emotional intelligence. As technology and society continue to advance, the way we understand and manage our emotions will also evolve.

One key area of focus in the future of emotional mastery is the integration of technology. There are already a number of apps and online tools available that aim to help individuals improve their emotional intelligence and manage their emotions more effectively. These tools use a variety of techniques such as mindfulness and cognitive-behavioral therapy to help users identify and change negative thought patterns, improve self-awareness, and increase emotional regulation.

Another area of focus is the use of artificial intelligence and machine learning to better understand and predict emotions. Researchers are currently exploring the use of AI-powered algorithms to analyze large amounts of data on human emotions in order to gain new insights into how emotions are generated and regulated in the brain. This could lead to the development of new techniques and tools for emotional mastery that are more personalized and effective.

Moreover, with the rise of remote work, emotional intelligence is becoming increasingly important in the workplace. As companies shift to a more virtual workforce, the ability to communicate and collaborate effectively in a digital environment is becoming more important. Employees will need to be able to manage their emotions in order to build and maintain relationships with colleagues, clients, and customers.

Finally, emotional mastery in the future will also include a better understanding of the impact of emotions on physical and mental health. Emotions have a direct impact on the body, influencing hormones and chemicals that affect health. This research will lead to better understanding of how to use emotions in a healthy way and how to prevent negative emotions from causing physical and mental health issues.

In conclusion, the future of emotional mastery is an exciting and rapidly-evolving field. With the integration of technology, advances in AI and machine learning, and a growing focus on emotional intelligence in the workplace, we can expect to see new and innovative approaches to managing our emotions in the years to come.

BONUS CHAPTER

Depression, Jealousy And Procrastination

Depression, jealousy, and procrastination are three common emotional challenges that many people struggle with. These emotions can be debilitating and can greatly impact one's ability to function in daily life.

DEPRESSION

Depression is a mental health disorder characterized by persistent feelings of sadness and loss of interest in activities. It is often accompanied by physical symptoms such as fatigue, changes in appetite and sleep patterns, and difficulty concentrating. The causes of depression are complex and varied, but it is believed to be related to a combination of genetic, environmental, and psychological factors. When it comes to the topic of depression, it is important to understand that it is a serious mental health condition that affects a large number of individuals. It can manifest in a variety of ways, including feelings of sadness, hopelessness, and a lack of interest in activities that were once enjoyed.

To curb depression, it is important to understand the underlying causes of the depression and address them directly. This may involve therapy or medication, but it may also involve lifestyle changes such as exercise, healthy eating, and stress management A combination of therapy and medication is the most effective way to treat depression. This can include cognitive behavioral therapy, talk therapy, and antidepressants.

Engaging in regular exercise, getting enough sleep, eating a healthy diet, and spending time with friends and loved ones can also help to manage and prevent depression.

JEALOUSY

Jealousy, on the other hand, is a complex emotion that often stems from feelings of insecurity or inadequacy. It is an emotional response to perceived threats to a valued relationship or possession. It can manifest in many different forms, from mild envy to intense rage, and can be directed towards people, objects, or even abstract concepts. Jealousy can be destructive and can cause relationship problems, but it can also be a motivator for personal growth and change.

To curb jealousy, it is important to focus on building self-esteem and self-confidence. This can be done by setting and achieving personal goals, practicing self-care, and surrounding oneself with supportive and positive people. Additionally, it is important to practice mindfulness and try to see things from a different perspective.

Jealousy can be addressed through therapy, particularly cognitive behavioral therapy, which can help to change negative thought patterns and behaviors that contribute to jealousy.

Practicing mindfulness and self-reflection, learning to communicate effectively, and building self-esteem can also help to manage and prevent jealousy.

PROCRASTINATION

Procrastination, the act of delaying or postponing tasks, is also an emotional challenge that many people face. It is often caused by fear, anxiety, or a lack of motivation. Procrastination can have negative effects on one's productivity and well-being, but it can be overcome by identifying the underlying causes and implementing strategies such as setting realistic goals, breaking tasks down into smaller chunks, and developing a sense of accountability.

To curb procrastination, it is important to break down large tasks into smaller, more manageable chunks. This can be done by setting specific and measurable goals and using time management techniques such as the Pomodoro Technique. Additionally, it is important to identify the underlying causes of procrastination, such as fear of failure, and work to overcome them.

Procrastination can be addressed through therapy, particularly cognitive behavioural therapy, which can help to change negative thought patterns and behaviours that contribute to procrastination.

Setting clear and specific goals, breaking down tasks into manageable chunks, and using time management strategies such as the Pomodoro Technique can help to manage and prevent procrastination.

In conclusion, emotional mastery is a lifelong journey that requires a deep understanding of one's emotions and the ability to effectively manage them. By learning to recognize and cope with common emotional challenges such as depression, jealousy, and procrastination, individuals can improve their emotional intelligence and lead more fulfilling lives. While these emotions can be difficult to manage, they can be overcome with the right approach and strategies. It is important to seek professional help if necessary and to remember that progress is not always linear and setbacks are a normal part of the process.

www.ingramcontent.com/pod-product-compliance
Lightning Source LLC
Chambersburg PA
CBHW071142220526
45467CB00015B/1707